I0409008

HOW TO CREATE IRRESISTIBLE OFFERS THAT CONVERT PROSPECTS INTO CUSTOMERS

STEPHEN STEPHENS

Copyright © 2023, STEPHEN STEPHENS
All rights reserved.

No part of this book may be reproduced, stored in a
retrieval system, or transmitted in any form or by
any means, electronic, mechanical, photocopying,
recording, scanning, or otherwise, without the prior
written permission of the publisher.

This book is sold subject to the condition that it
shall not, by way of trade or otherwise, be lent,
re-sold, hired out, or otherwise circulated without
the publisher's prior consent in any form of binding
or cover other than that in which it is published and
without a similar condition including this condition
being imposed on the subsequent purchaser.

1

TABLE OF CONTENT

INTRODUCTION

Nothing feels the same when everything starts working for good after the struggles. I know this because I've been there. I've been through the pain of failure, the frustration of rejection, and the despair of feeling like I would never succeed. But I also know the joy of success, the satisfaction of knowing that all my hard work paid off, and the sense of fulfillment that comes from helping others.

I learned how to create irresistible offers through trial and error. I read books, attended seminars, and talked to experts. But the most important thing I did was experiment. I tried different things, and I kept track of what worked and what didn't.

I learned that the key to creating an irresistible offer is to understand your target audience. What are their needs and wants? What are their pain points? What motivates them? Once you understand your target audience, you can create an offer that speaks to them directly.

You also need to make sure your offer is clear, concise, and easy to understand. People don't have time to read through a lot of fine print. They want to know what you're offering, and they want to know what's in it for them.

Finally, you need to make sure your offer is valuable. People are more likely to buy something if they believe they're getting a good deal. So make sure your offer is worth their time and money.

Creating irresistible offers is not easy. It takes time, effort, and trial and error. But it's worth it. When you can create an offer that people can't resist, you'll be well on your way to success.

I'm writing this book to share everything I know about creating irresistible offers. I want to help you achieve your goals and make a difference in the world. I know that you can do it. So what are you waiting for?

Start creating irresistible offers today!

1

COMPREHENDING YOUR TARGET MARKET

Marketers are frequently so focused on selling their products or services that they neglect to understand their target market. This can be an expensive mistake, resulting in unsuccessful marketing strategies that waste critical time and money.

Making assumptions about your target market is easy, but it can be a deadly mistake. Assumptions can lead to off-target and unproductive marketing strategies.

Doing research is the first step in knowing your target market. This involves knowing their demographics, psychographics, and purchasing habits.

Your target market's demographics are the qualities of the people who are most likely to purchase your goods or service. Age, gender, income, education, location, and interests are examples of such traits.

It might be tough to determine who your target market is if you are new to a market. Talking to your target market is the best approach to understanding them. Inquire about their wants, needs, and pain points. Keep an eye on what your competitors are doing to achieve their target audience.

- What do they do well?
- What could they have done better?
- Keep an eye out for the latest trends affecting your target market.
- What are they on about?
- What do they care about?

You can utilize this knowledge to generate marketing messages that will resonate with your target market if you have a clear grasp of them. You can also utilize this data to create products and services that meet their requirements.

Even if you're new to the industry, there are numerous locations where you may find the demographics of your target market.

Many governments collect information on their residents, including demographic data. This information is frequently available online. Industry groups frequently gather information about their members, including demographic data. This information is frequently made available to the general public.
Market research companies acquire consumer data, including demographic information. This information is frequently offered for purchase.

You may obtain a better grasp of your target market and design marketing messages that will resonate with them by utilizing these resources. You can also utilize this data to create products and services that meet their requirements.

Not knowing your target market's exact needs can have a lot of negative repercussions on your organization, including resource waste, missed opportunities, and, most importantly, brand damage. Talking to your target market is the best approach to understanding them. Inquire about their wants, needs, and pain points.

This can be accomplished by surveys, interviews, or focus groups. Being a good listener is another technique to detect someone's pain points. When someone is speaking to you, pay close attention to what they are saying. Pay close attention to their words, tone of voice, and body language. This will assist you in understanding how they truly feel and what is important to them.

To determine someone's pain points, ask questions. When you ask someone a question, you demonstrate an interest in what they have to say. You are also allowing them to express their views and feelings to you. Body language can be an effective means of communicating emotions. Pay attention to someone's body language when you're talking to them.

- Are they twitching?
- Is it possible that they are avoiding eye contact?
- Do they have their arms crossed?

These are all indications that they are uneasy or stressed. Paying attention to your surroundings pays well.

- What is everyone talking about?
- What are they upset about?
- What are their difficulties?

Being watchful allows you to obtain insight into the problems that people are facing.

You can utilize this knowledge to generate marketing messages that will resonate with your target market if you have a clear grasp of them. You can also utilize this data to create products and services that meet their requirements.

Several internet tools can assist you in determining the needs and desires of your target market. These programs frequently allow you to search for data based on demographics, interests, and other parameters. Attending industry events allows you to meet people in your business and learn about their target consumers.

These events can also be used to network with new consumers. Articles regarding target markets are common in industry magazines. These articles might provide you with vital insights into your target market's needs and desires.
There are numerous online forums and groups where people from various markets can discuss and share information.

A good example is social media. Social networking is an excellent approach to engaging with people from various markets. You can utilize social media to inform potential clients about your products or services and to solicit feedback. Attending industry events is an excellent method to meet people from other markets. These events can also be used to network with new consumers.

You can connect with people from other markets if you have your website or blog. You can post information about your products or services as well as solicit feedback from prospective clients.

Once you've discovered someone's pain points, you can use that knowledge to assist them. Put yourself in the shoes of the other person.
- What are they thinking?
- What are they experiencing?
You can better grasp their problems if you are empathic. Building trust and rapport with someone may take time. They will be more willing to open up

to you and express their concerns once you have earned their trust. When someone confides in you about their problems, you must remain confidential. Do not give out their personal information to anyone else.

You can provide them with assistance, advice, or a solution to their situation. You can also utilize this data to create goods or services that assist customers in overcoming their pain areas.

The next step is to research your intended audience. This can assist you in better understanding your target market. When researching your target market, are you making the faults of not completing enough research, not asking the proper questions, and not acting on your research findings?

Surveys, interviews, and focus groups are all effective methods for researching your target market. If you're unfamiliar with the terms direct and indirect surveys, direct surveys ask respondents to contribute information about themselves or their experiences directly. In contrast, indirect surveys ask respondents to provide information about individuals or hypothetical circumstances.

Direct surveys are an excellent technique to gather quantitative information about your target market. Use various question types. A variety of closed-ended, open-ended, and scaled questions should be asked. Keep your surveys brief and simple to complete. People are more likely to finish a survey if it is brief and simple.

Provide a prize for completing the survey. This could include a discount, a free product, or the opportunity to win a prize.

You can also inquire about their buying habits and level of satisfaction with your products or services.

Indirect surveys are another excellent technique to gather qualitative information about your target market. Make use of a range of prompts. To convey their thoughts and feelings, ask them to write, draw, or create something.

Be open to many interpretations. An indirect survey question has no right or incorrect response.To interpret the results, use a focus group. A focus group might assist you in comprehending the significance of the facts. You can inquire about their views, feelings, and experiences by asking open-ended inquiries. You can also inquire about their objectives and aspirations.

Direct interviews are an excellent approach to learning more about your target market. Prepare yourself. Conduct research and make a list of questions to ask. Be an attentive listener. Pay attention to what the other person is saying and offer follow-up questions as well as take notes. This will assist you in remembering the key points of the interview. You can inquire about their personal life, professional lives, and hobbies. You might also inquire about their aspirations, dreams, and concerns.

Focus groups are an excellent approach to gathering input from a diverse range of individuals on your products or services. Gather a varied collection of people. This will allow you to gain a variety of viewpoints. Establish ground rules. This will help to guarantee that the conversation is fruitful. Be a connector. It is your responsibility to keep the discussion on course and to ensure that everyone gets an opportunity to participate. Take careful notes. This will assist you in remembering the key aspects of the talk.

You can show them prototypes, interrogate them, and gauge their reactions.
You can gain a more thorough view of your target market by using some research approaches. This data can assist you in developing products and services that fulfill their requirements and desires.

However, it is also important to create a buyer persona. If you don't know who your target customers are, your marketing messages will be less likely to reach them. This can result in lost sales since you're not successfully targeting your marketing messages, you'll likely waste money on advertising that doesn't reach your target clients, and you'll be less likely to deliver the kind of care they expect if you don't understand their demands.

Customer discontent and turnover might result from this. A buyer persona is a fictitious portrayal of your ideal customer. It should include demographic information, needs, wants, and pain areas. It's also a fictitious depiction of your ideal customer. It is founded on research and data about your current and prospective clients. Buyer personas assist you in better understanding your target audience so that you can produce marketing and sales communications that are relevant to them.

This is because you already understand how to determine your target market. What are the demographics of your target market, what are their needs and desires, what are their alleged pain areas, and how do you research your target market?

Develop a buyer persona.
A buyer persona is a fictitious portrayal of your ideal customer. It should include demographic information, needs, wants, and pain areas. Create marketing messages that are relevant to your buyer persona.

If you want to establish a persona for your firm, you need to start with research. You must first conduct research to understand your target demographic before creating a buyer persona. Surveys, interviews, and focus groups may be used in this research. Be as specific as possible when establishing your buyer persona. This includes details about their demographics, requirements, desires, and pain spots.

Buyer personas can be used to instruct sales professionals on how to approach potential clients most effectively. If your target persona is a small business owner, you may teach your salespeople about the specific issues that small business owners encounter and how your product or service can assist them in overcoming those challenges. Buyer personas can help guide product development decisions.

If your target persona is a millennial, you should think about creating a product or service that is specifically suited for millennials. All of this adds up to better marketing and sales effectiveness:

Buyer personas may assist you in developing marketing and sales communications that are more effective at reaching and converting your target demographic.
Increase the success of your product development and client pleasure.

Your marketing communications should be targeted to the demands and desires of your buyer persona. Analyze the outcomes of your marketing activities. Monitor the effectiveness of your marketing activities to determine how successfully you are reaching your target market.

Furthermore, buyer personas can be utilized to create marketing messages that are personalized to the needs and desires of your target audience. If your target persona is a busy working mom, you should learn about their daily schedule so that you can produce marketing messages that emphasize the convenience and time-saving aspects of your product or service.

Use real facts from your study to create your buyer persona. This will assist you in developing a more true and realistic persona.
Your buyer persona should be a live document that you keep up to date. As your target audience changes, this will ensure that it remains accurate and relevant.

You may better understand your target customer and generate marketing and sales messages that speak to their needs and desires by creating buyer personas.

You can now construct a buyer persona and create marketing messages that will resonate with your target demographic.

Because you have identified your target market's needs and desires. What qualities do they seek in a product or service? What are their annoyances? What are their reasons?

Make use of your knowledge of your target market to generate marketing messages that respond to their needs and desires. Use language that they will understand and resonate with. Make certain that your marketing messages are matched to the demographics of your target market. Consider their age, gender, income, level of education, and location. Use visuals that are appealing to your target audience. Consider their hobbies, interests, and way of life.

Check that your marketing messages are in line with your brand. Your marketing communications should be consistent with your brand's overall look and feel. Here's an example of how you may leverage your knowledge about your target market to produce marketing messages that speak to them. Assume you own a company that offers organic dog food. Your target market consists of pet owners who are concerned about their pets' health. You understand that your target market is likely to be a female in her 30s or 40s with a college degree, a higher-than-average income, and a residence in a big city.

You may utilize this information to generate marketing messages that respond to the needs and desires of your target market. You may, for example, design a marketing message emphasizing the health benefits of organic dog food. You might also employ visually appealing visuals that appeal to your target demographic, such as images of happy, healthy dogs.

You may produce marketing messages that are more likely to resonate with your target demographic if you follow these recommendations. This will assist you in raising brand awareness, generating leads, and increasing sales. Never, ever forget humor is an excellent tool for connecting with your target audience and making your marketing messaging more remembered. But tales sell, and people love stories, so utilize them to sell your business and connect emotionally with your target market.

Numerous types of stories may be told in marketing, but some of the more effective ones are as follows. The most effective are brand tales, customer stories, testimonial stories, and case study evaluations.

Brand tales are fantastic stories about your brand, its beginnings, and its aim. They can help to emotionally link your brand with your target audience and make them feel like they're a part of something bigger.

Customer tales are stories that share your customers' experiences with your target audience. They can assist in establishing trust and credibility with your target audience and demonstrating the benefits of your products or services.
Testimonial tales are stories that include consumer testimonials regarding their experiences with your products or services. They can be an effective

technique to demonstrate the worth of your products or services to your target audience.

Case study tales describe how your products or services assisted individual clients in achieving their objectives. They can be an excellent approach to demonstrate to your target audience how your products or services can assist them in achieving their objectives.

When deciding on a tale to convey, examine your target audience and what would resonate with them. You should also ensure that the story is authentic and credible.

Follow one simple rule: look for personal and relatable stories. People are more inclined to connect with stories to which they can personally relate. Seek out stories with a clear emotional narrative. The story should begin with a problem, progress to a climax, and then address the problem.

Look for well-written and compelling content. The story should be simple to read and grasp, and it should hold the reader's attention from start to finish.

As long as you've sold a product, you can uncover emotive stories that will connect with your audience and help you meet your marketing objectives.

Never forget to be genuine. People can detect a fake a mile away, so be genuine in your marketing efforts. Allow your personality to shine through and demonstrate to your target market that you are genuine people that care about their requirements.

Finally, track the outcomes of your marketing efforts. Monitor the effectiveness of your marketing activities to determine how successfully you are reaching your target market.

Setting goals is essential before you begin measuring your results. What do you hope to accomplish with your marketing efforts? Do you want to build brand awareness, generate leads, or enhance sales?

Once you've determined your objectives, you must select the appropriate metrics to monitor. You may track a variety of KPIs, including website traffic, social media interaction, and lead creation.

There are numerous tracking solutions accessible, including Google Analytics and HubSpot. Google Analytics is a free tool for tracking website traffic, social media activity, and other important information.

Adobe Analytics and HubSpot are paid marketing solutions that include website tracking, social media management, and lead generation.

These tools can assist you in tracking website traffic, social media interaction, and other important metrics like Lead Generation Rate, Cost Per Lead, Return on Marketing Investment, Customer Acquisition Cost, and Time on Page. This will assist you in determining what is and is not functioning.

After tracking your outcomes, you may need to make changes to your marketing efforts. This could include altering your target audience, messaging, or budget.

If you're not reaching your intended audience, you might want to reconsider. This could include altering your messaging, budget, or marketing platforms. That problem might be your message. If your messaging isn't connecting with your target audience, you may need to revise it. This could include altering the tone of your messaging, the language you employ, or the content you provide.

Best of all, if you aren't receiving the desired outcomes, you may need to increase your spending. This may enable you to reach a larger audience, employ more effective marketing methods, or develop more compelling content.

If your organization is spending a lot of money on Facebook advertising but not seeing a corresponding rise in sales, it might think about investing in other marketing channels, such as search engine optimization (SEO) or email marketing. If you aren't getting the desired results, you may need to rethink your marketing channels. This might include using multiple social media sites, running different types of ads, or attending different events, and you should already know where your clients live based on your customer persona.

2

ESTIMATE THE VALUE
OF YOUR OFFER

In today's competitive environment, being able to identify the value of your service is more critical than ever. Many people, however, struggle with this duty. They don't understand their target market, can't differentiate their offering from the competitors, and don't know how to properly explain the value of their service.

Don't be concerned if you're experiencing any of these issues. You're not by yourself. But don't give up hope. There are alternatives. By following the advice I provide, you can begin to establish the value of your service and position yourself as an industry leader.

After you've determined who your target audience is. What are their wants and requirements, as well as their pain points? It is preferable to identify the advantages of your service. What issues does your offer address? What advantages does it provide? If you don't grasp the benefits of your products and are only interested in making money, you're doing it wrong because that's what new marketers do. It is not sufficient to simply have an excellent product. You must be able to describe the benefits of your product in a way that your target audience will understand.

You may discover the benefits of your offer and begin communicating them to your target audience in a way that they will understand. This will assist you in increasing sales and growing your firm.

Ask your consumers what they enjoy about your product and what benefits they've gotten from utilizing it. Look at what other people are saying about your product. What advantages are they emphasizing? Consider your competition. What advantages do they provide? How can you make your product stand out?

You may produce a more appealing sales message and attract more clients by taking the time to identify the benefits of your offer. Consider your offer's characteristics and benefits. What issues does it address? What advantages does it provide? How will it improve your customers' lives?
If you're selling software, you might emphasize features like usability, scalability, and security. If you're marketing a service, you might emphasize ease, customer service, and expertise.

Compare your offer to similar market products or services. What are the main distinctions? What are the advantages and disadvantages of each option? Once you've identified your offer's characteristics and benefits, you should compare it to similar items or services on the market. This can assist you understand how your offer compares to the competition.

When evaluating your deal, examine elements such as pricing, features, advantages, and customer service. The advantages are what truly determine your price because customers don't care about the qualities of a product; all they care about is what it has to offer them. You should also examine the company's reputation while purchasing a product or service. Consider your own customer experience. In the past, what variables affected your decision to purchase a product or service? What did you search for in those offerings in terms of value?

Do not just state that your offer is "valuable." Describe how it will benefit your consumers. Provide evidence to back up your arguments. For example, you could use client feedback or industry studies, but anecdotes are ideal in this situation. To persuade your customers that your offer is worthwhile, use clear and succinct wording.

Conduct some self-research. What were your needs and desires that drove you to create this product? What was the source of your discomfort? What were you prepared to pay for? When attempting to explain the value of your offer, consider your personal experience as a consumer. In the past, what variables affected your decision to purchase a product or service? What did you search for in those offerings in terms of value?

Consider your own experience to gain a better grasp of what clients are looking for. This will assist you in positioning your offer appealingly to your target audience. Get feedback from industry professionals. What are their thoughts on the worth of your offer? What suggestions do they have for you?
Getting feedback from industry professionals is usually a good idea. What are their thoughts on the worth of your offer? What suggestions do they have for you?

You might acquire a new perspective on your offer by soliciting comments from specialists. This input can assist you in improving your offering and making it more valuable to your clients.

By taking into account all of these elements, you can begin to gain a better sense of the worth of your offer. This will assist you in positioning your item and pricing it in a way that is appealing to your target audience.

When analyzing the features and benefits of your offer, consider how they will affect your clients. Are you making the greatest choice for your circumstances? It's easy to get caught up in a product's or service's features, but it's crucial to remember that features are only tools. The real question is, how will these tools assist you in reaching your objectives? Remember to compare apples to apples, factor in the cost, and read the fine print. You can ensure that you are making the finest selection for your circumstances. What issues will they address? What problems will they solve? How will they improve your customers' lives?

Once you understand the difficulties your solution solves and the benefits it provides, you can begin to explain these to your target audience in a way that they will comprehend. This will assist you in increasing sales and growing your firm.

Consider weight loss products.
   The issue is that you desire to lose weight. Benefit is that our weight reduction program can assist you in losing weight in a safe and effective manner.
   You're having difficulty learning a new language. Our language learning program can assist you in learning a new language swiftly and easily. The issue is that you are worried and overloaded.
   Advantage is that our stress management program can assist you in reducing stress and improving your general well-being.

You may design a more compelling sales message and attract more clients by recognizing the challenges your solution solves and the benefits it provides. You can design a more appealing sales message and attract more clients by taking the time to discover the problems your solution solves and the benefits it provides.

It can be tough to quantify the worth of my offer. It can be difficult to assess the impact of my offer, compare it to others, and decide its exact value in your particular scenario. However, it is critical to attempt to quantify the value of my offer so that you can make an informed judgment about whether it is appropriate for you. How much money will you save your consumers with your offer? How much time will they save?

How much stress will it take away? Determine the expenditures that your offer can help your consumers save. This could include product, service, time, or resource costs.

Calculate how much time your offer will save your clients. This could include time spent looking for information, making decisions, or finishing tasks. Consider how much tension your offer can alleviate for your customers. This could entail dealing with problems, making blunders, or feeling overwhelmed.

For example, a software company selling a CRM system could estimate the value of its offering by estimating how much time it can save its customers. For example, if the CRM system saves a customer 10 hours per week, the corporation could claim that its product saves the customer $5,200 per year (based on a $52 hourly pay).

A corporation that sells a weight reduction program could estimate the amount of money it can save its consumers to measure the value of its offer. For example, if the weight reduction program assists a customer in losing 10 pounds, the corporation may claim that its service will save the customer $500 in medical expenses (based on the typical cost of obesity-related medical bills).

A corporation that sells a stress management program could estimate the amount of stress that it can relieve for its consumers to measure the value of its offer. For example, if the stress management program assists a client in reducing their stress levels by 20%, the corporation may claim that its offer improves the customer's overall health and well-being.

You may build a more appealing sales pitch, attract more clients, and begin to create benefits that are relevant to your target audience by quantifying the worth of your offer. It is critical to understand the customer's demands and effectively express the benefits of the offer while communicating an offer. One method is to quantify the benefits. For example, if your offer can save your consumers $100 per year, you may include a benefit that states, "Our product can save you $100 per year." Customers will be more likely to take action if they grasp the value of your offer.

Overselling is one issue that frequently goes unnoticed. When you oversell your offer, the buyer may be disappointed if they do not obtain all of the benefits that were promised. Not being prepared to answer inquiries can give the consumer the impression that they are not being taken seriously, which can cause them to lose interest in the offer.

Make certain that the value of your product is properly communicated in your marketing materials. Use clear and succinct language, and emphasize the benefits of your offer.

Concentrate on the advantages your offer delivers. Don't merely discuss the benefits of your product or service. Instead, concentrate on the advantages your offer will deliver to your clients. For example, rather than suggesting your product is "easy to use," say it will "save you time."

Use simple, direct language. The use of jargon or technical terminology that your target audience may not understand is discouraged. Instead, utilize plain, straightforward language that your target audience will comprehend.

Make your point. Do not simply state that your product is "good." Instead, be clear about the advantages it provides. For example, rather than claiming your product is "helpful," mention it will "help you save money."

Make use of storytelling. Stories are more likely to be remembered and persuaded than facts and data. When discussing the benefits of your product, utilize tales to demonstrate how your product has aided others.

Make use of testimonies. Testimonials from satisfied and happy customers can be an effective approach to conveying the value of your offer. When using testimonials, make sure that they are relevant to your target audience and illustrate the benefits of your offer. Testimonials from satisfied customers can be an effective approach to demonstrating the worth of your offer.

Provide a free trial or demo. A free trial or demo allows potential clients to experience your product or service before purchasing it. This allows them to see the worth of your offer directly.

Make a money-back guarantee available. A money-back guarantee can provide potential consumers peace of mind, knowing that if they are dissatisfied with your goods or service, they can get their money back.

Make use of graphics. Visuals can be an effective tool for communicating the value of your service. When employing graphics, make sure they are of good quality and demonstrate the benefits of your service.

A CRM system vendor may claim that its software saves customers time by automating chores and offering insights into customer behavior. A new software program may benefit customers by saving them time and money. A consulting service may provide the benefit of assisting consumers in resolving a specific problem.

A corporation selling a weight reduction program can claim that its product can help customers lose weight by providing diet plans, exercise regimens, and expert support. A weight reduction program may benefit clients by assisting them in losing weight and improving their health.

Meanwhile, a corporation selling a stress management program can claim that its product can help clients reduce stress by offering relaxation techniques, meditation exercises, and access to a community of other stressed-out people.

Make certain that your marketing materials reflect your brand's identity. Customers should be able to identify your firm and its products or services if your marketing materials mirror the appearance and feel of your brand.

To reach your target demographic, use a range of marketing methods. Because not everyone responds to the same marketing messaging, it's critical to reach your target demographic through a number of channels. You could employ email marketing, social media marketing, or paid advertising, for example.

Keep track of your results and alter your plan as necessary. It's critical to track the results of your marketing activities so you can determine what works and what doesn't. This will allow you to tweak your plan as necessary to improve your outcomes.

3

INSTILL A SENSE OF
URGENCY

Marketers face a difficult task when it comes to instilling a sense of urgency. Customers will tune them out if they utilize urgency tactics too frequently. Customers may not take action if there is no sense of urgency. The goal is to strike a balance and utilize urgency tactics sparingly and only when they are truly necessary.

Creating a sense of urgency is an effective technique to push others to act. People are more likely to prioritize chores and make speedy judgments when they feel a feeling of urgency. This can be a useful tool in many situations, including business, education, and personal life.

When it came to marketing my items, I used to struggle with establishing a sense of urgency. I would frequently write emails or make phone calls to customers, but I would rarely receive a response. I was irritated and had no idea what I was doing wrong.

I was talking to a friend who was also a salesperson one day. He advised me that if I wanted to close more sales, I needed to generate a sense of urgency. He advised me to identify the benefits of acting swiftly, to make the benefits plain and succinct, to emphasize the urgency of the situation, and to personalize the message.

I took his advice and began using the four-step approach. I began by identifying the advantages of acting promptly. For example, I would inform them that if they bought my goods right now, they could save money or receive a free gift.

The benefits were then made clear and concise. I would eliminate jargon and use straightforward language. I would also make certain that the benefits were pertinent to the customer's needs.

I then emphasized the importance of the circumstance. Customers would be told that my goods were in high demand or that the promotion was only available for a short period.
The message was then customized. I'd address the consumer by name and use language geared to their individual requirements.

I noticed a difference in my results once I began using the four-step procedure. I was increasing my sales and closing more deals. I was finally able to generate urgency and sell my stuff.

You can also instill a sense of urgency in your clients, encouraging them to act and purchase your items or services. When you use terms like "now," "limited time," and "deadline," you convey a sense of immediacy. "Sign up now for our limited-time offer!" for example, or "Act now before the deadline expires!"

Highlight the advantages of acting swiftly. People are more willing to act swiftly when they comprehend the rewards of doing so. You may say, "If you sign up today, you'll get a free gift!" or "If you act now, you'll save 50%!"
A company that sells online courses may provide a limited-time discount. "Get 50% off our online courses for the next 24 hours only!" the corporation could say.
A blog that offers marketing advice may provide a free ebook on how to expand your business. The

blog could include phrases such as, "Get our free ebook on how to grow your business!" This promotion is only valid for the next week." A software company may provide a free trial of its product. "Try our software for free for 30 days!" the corporation may say. There is no need for a credit card."

Step 1: What are the benefits that people will receive if they act now? For example, if you are marketing a product, you could emphasize that clients can save money by purchasing immediately. If you're selling a service, you may emphasize the fact that they can get started right now. Make your message unique. When you customize your message, you give the impression that you are communicating personally to them. This can aid in instilling a sense of urgency. For instance, you could remark, "I know you're interested in this offer, so don't pass it up!" Sign up now!"When people see others acting, they are more likely to follow suit. "Thousands of people have already signed up!" or "This offer is so popular, it's selling out fast!" Never forget to set a firm deadline. People must be aware of the deadline in order to act. "This offer is only good for the next 24 hours!" or "The deadline to sign up is Friday, March 1st!" Always keep the deadline in mind. People may forget about a deadline that is too far away. People may feel rushed if the deadline is too tight, and they may make a decision they later regret. One emotion that allows people to sell more is regret.

Step 2: Make the benefits as clear and succinct as possible. People should be able to rapidly understand the benefits of acting without having to read a lot of material. Avoid jargon and use straightforward, concise language.

Highlight the advantages of acting swiftly. People are more willing to act swiftly when they comprehend the rewards of doing so. You may say, "If you sign up today, you'll get a free gift!" or "If you act now, you'll save 50%!"
Make use of customer testimonials from delighted and happy consumers. When people observe how others have benefited from swift action, they are more likely to follow suit.

Step 3: Emphasize the gravity of the problem. People must recognize that there is a finite window of opportunity to act. This can be accomplished by using time-sensitive phrasing such as "limited time offer" or "act now."
People are more prone to feel a sense of urgency when they perceive something to be scarce. This is because they don't want to pass up the opportunity.
 Scarcity can also cause FOMO (fear of missing out).
A perfect approach I produce for FOMO is not to tell individuals that if they don't buy now, they won't be able to buy later; this doesn't work on prospects who see your stuff all the time. "It is a very busy time of year for us, and people are already getting ready for the year's end rush." That is where remorse comes into play. People are concerned that if they don't act quickly, they will miss out on something they desire.
 Scarcity can also be exciting. This is because people feel ecstatic about the chance to have something rare.

Scarcity can be used in marketing to tap into these emotions and increase sales. However, it is critical to use scarcity in an ethical and open manner. You should never mislead your prospects or make them feel compelled to buy something they don't desire. This will make them feel special and increase their likelihood of taking advantage of them.

When using Fomo, having social proof as a backup will give you a significant advantage. When people see others acting, they are more likely to follow suit. "Thousands of people have already signed up!" or "This offer is so popular, it's selling out fast!"
Another technique to generate a sense of urgency is to provide a limited-time discount or bonus. People are more likely to respond swiftly if they know they can save money or obtain something extra. "Get 20% off your purchase today!" or "Sign up for our email list and get a free gift!" are two examples.

Another technique to establish a sense of urgency is to set a deadline for taking action. People are more likely to act when they are aware that they have a limited amount of time to do so. "This offer is only good for the next 24 hours!" or "The deadline to sign up is Friday, March 1st!"

You can generate a sense of urgency and push others to act by employing these tactics. This can be a useful tool in many situations, including business, education, and personal life.
To encourage people to buy soon, a company may provide a limited-time discount on its products or services. To ensure that students stay on track, a school may establish a deadline for them to finish tasks.

A personal trainer may provide a complimentary consultation to encourage clients to begin exercising. Using these tactics, you may generate a sense of urgency and encourage people to act.

Make use of time-sensitive language. When you use terms like "now," "limited time," and "deadline," you convey a sense of immediacy. "Sign up now for our limited-time offer!" for example, or "Act now before the deadline expires!"

Provide a substantial discount or incentive. People are more likely to act if they believe they can save money or obtain something extra. For example, you could provide a 20% discount on your products or services, or you may provide a free gift with a purchase.

Make the offer or bonus time-limited. People are more likely to act if they know they can only get a discount or bonus for a short time. "Get 20% off your purchase today only!" or "Sign up for our email list and receive a free gift for the first 100 people who sign up!"

Step 4: Customize the message. People are more likely to act if they believe the message is directed specifically at them. You can customize the message by addressing their special needs or utilizing their name. "Action now and save 50%!"

"This offer is only good for the next 24 hours."

"Only for a limited time! Begin right away."

"We're so sure you'll love our product that we're offering a money-back guarantee."

"Don't pass up this opportunity!" Sign up now." these are some instances of how to emphasize the benefits of acting promptly.

Businesses may generate a sense of urgency and inspire customers to act by employing time-sensitive language. This can result in more sales, leads, and visitors to your website. Instill a sense of scarcity. People are more likely to want something when they believe it is scarce. For example, you could state, "Only 100 spots are available!" or "This offer is only good today!"
Use social proof so that when people see others acting, they are more inclined to follow suit. "Thousands of people have already signed up!" or "This offer is so popular, it's selling out fast!"

Provide a free trial or demo. This allows individuals to try your goods or service before committing to anything. Make it simple for people to act. People are more likely to act when it is simple for them to do so. Use clear and straightforward instructions, and provide various options for action.

Scarcity is an effective marketing tactic for increasing sales. People are more likely to want something when they believe it is scarce. This is due to scarcity instilling a sense of urgency and the dread of missing out.
Take advantage of limited-time specials. For a short period, offer your products or services at a reduced price. This will generate a sense of urgency, increasing the likelihood that people will buy today.
Use only a small amount. Only sell a few of your products or services. People will feel compelled to act quickly in order to avoid missing out.
Set up a waiting list. Create a waiting list if your product or service is in high demand. This will make individuals feel special and as if they are receiving something special. Share limited-time

bargains and limited-quantity products on social media. When sharing these offers on social media, use clear and succinct language that emphasizes the scarcity. For example, "This offer is only available for the next 24 hours!" or "Only 100 units left!"

Send forth special deals to your subscribers using email marketing. When you send out unique offers to your subscribers, make it clear that they are the first to learn about these deals.

4

MAKE PURCHASING SIMPLE

Making their items difficult to purchase is a common mistake made by marketers. This can be accomplished by overcomplicating the checkout process, offering too many payment alternatives, refusing to offer free delivery, failing to provide clear and succinct product descriptions, failing to provide high-quality photographs and videos, and failing to create trust with their audience.

I have a friend who got into information marketing in 2016. John was an information marketer who was having difficulty selling his items. He had a terrific product, but he was having difficulties selling it. He was frustrated and unsure of what to do. While spending money on advertisements yet having no dialogue. He asked if I was available for a coffee sometime. As a buddy, I concurred when John shared his difficulties over coffee. I went to John's website and noticed that the checkout process was overly cumbersome. I also noted that John did not provide free shipping.

I advised John that he should make it easier for consumers to purchase his products. I suggested he streamline the checkout process and provide free shipping. John took my suggestions and implemented the improvements I proposed. He streamlined the checkout procedure and began giving free shipping. John began selling more things as a result of my assistance. He is still grateful for the coffee time we shared.

The first step in getting someone to buy your goods is to make them easy to find. Which John did admirably, but not everyone can. This entails establishing a strong online presence and listing your product on major online marketplaces. You should also spend on search engine optimization (SEO) to ensure that your product appears toward the top of search results.

Make your website search engine friendly. This includes including relevant keywords and phrases in your website's content, titles, and meta descriptions. If you sell shoes, for example, you may include keywords like "running shoes," "sneakers," or "athletic shoes." To identify the proper keywords, you can utilize a tool like Google Search Console.

Produce high-quality material. Blog posts, articles, infographics, and videos might all be included. The idea is to develop content for your target audience that is useful, interesting, and relevant. If you sell shoes, for example, you might write a blog post about the various types of running shoes or make a video about how to find the best running shoes for your needs.

Guest writing on other websites can also be an excellent approach to exposing your brand and products to a new audience. Make sure to provide a link back to your own website when you guest write. For example, you could create a blog post for a fitness website about the necessity of working out in the proper shoes.

Implement social media campaigns. This could include sharing your items on social media, holding contests, or collaborating with influencers. For example, you could hold an Instagram contest in which people may enter to win a pair of running shoes.

Attending industry events might help you meet potential clients and partners. Before attending any event, do your homework and learn everything you can about the event and the individuals who will be there. This will allow you to make the most of your event time and meet the right individuals.

When attending an event, it is critical to create goals for yourself. What do you want to gain from your attendance at the event? Do you wish to meet new prospective clients? Do you want to hear about new industry trends? Do you wish to meet other professionals? Having specific objectives can help you stay focused and make the most of your time at the event.

After you've established your objectives, it's time to start planning for the event. Make sure you have your business cards and brochures available, and that you have a strategy for introducing yourself and starting talks.

When you meet individuals at events, you should be prepared to talk about your company. Prepare a concise elevator pitch that describes what your company does and why it is special. Be excited and passionate about your company, and be ready to answer any questions that may arise.

It's critical to follow up with the folks you meet after the event. Send them a thank-you note and express your want to collaborate again. You can also take advantage of this time to learn more about their company and see if there are any ways you can assist each other. First impressions are crucial, so dress properly when attending gatherings. This will demonstrate to others that you are serious about your business and worth their time.

If you are nice and approachable, people are more likely to want to talk to you. Make eye contact, smile, and be receptive to conversation.

Be an excellent listener when you're chatting to others. In order to demonstrate that you are interested in what they have to say, ask questions. Building relationships takes time. Expect to meet the right individuals and close deals slowly. You will eventually attain your goals if you are patient and persistent. When attending events, keep business cards and brochures on hand. You may go to a running expo and meet folks who are looking to buy running shoes.

Make use of paid advertising, such as Google AdWords, Facebook Ads, or LinkedIn Ads. Paid advertising can be an excellent approach to immediately reach a big number of individuals. You might conduct a Google AdWords ad targeting those who are looking for "running shoes."

Use product names that are straightforward and succinct. By reading the name of your product, customers should be able to easily comprehend what it is. Instead of "The Ultimate Running Shoe," you may call your product "The Runner's Shoe."

Make use of high-resolution product photos and videos. Customers should be able to see how your product appears and functions. A video of someone running in your product could be included.

Customers must grasp what your product is, what it accomplishes, and why they require it. You may create a product description that details the advantages of your product for runners. Make a money-back guarantee available. Customers will have peace of mind knowing that they can get their money back if they are dissatisfied with your product. For instance, you may provide a 30-day money-back guarantee on all of your products.

Provide outstanding client service. Customers should be able to access support promptly and simply if they have any queries or problems. You may provide 24-hour customer service via phone, email, or live chat.

Once potential clients have discovered your product, you must ensure that it is simple to understand. This includes clear and succinct product descriptions as well as high-quality photos and videos. You should also include thorough product information, such as features, benefits, and technical specs. The final stage is to make it simple for prospective clients to purchase your product. This includes accepting credit cards, debit cards, PayPal, and Google Pay as payment methods. You should also provide free or low-cost shipping. You can also make it easier for people to buy your product by offering discounts, coupons, and promotions. You may also generate a sense of urgency by running limited-time offers or flash sales.

Provide a simple checkout process. The checkout procedure should be straightforward and simple. Customers should be able to swiftly and simply submit their payment information and shipping address. Amazon's checkout process is among the best in the business. It is simple to use, safe, and efficient. Customers may check out quickly and effortlessly with only a few clicks. You can use that as a starting point.

Customers should be able to access support promptly and simply if they have any queries or problems. You should provide 24-hour customer service by phone, email, or live chat.

Customers are more likely to purchase from businesses they trust. Maintain a good brand reputation for your firm by providing exceptional products and services and responding to consumer comments.

5

TEST AND IMPROVE
YOUR OFFER

It is critical to refine and test your offer before launching it. Without it, you risk squandering your time and money on an offer that does not appeal to your target demographic. Low conversion rates, a lack of clarity and appeal, and uncompetitive pricing are some of the drawbacks of not refining and testing your offer. To avoid these problems, it is critical to first define your target demographic, then develop a clear and compelling offer and test it with a small group of potential buyers. You can improve and test your offer by following these suggestions.

When evaluating your offers, it is critical to test a range of versions. This will assist you in determining which offer will best resonate with your target demographic. Gathering enough data to make informed decisions about your offers takes time. Don't give up on an offer that isn't functioning well too soon. Allow some time to see if it improves.

Once you've collected data from your tests, you must properly analyze it. This will assist you in determining the elements influencing your outcomes.

Failure to make changes based on facts could cost you. Once you've identified the factors influencing your outcomes, you must act quickly to make modifications to your offer based on that information. This is the only method to gradually enhance your outcomes.

When evaluating your offers, aim to test at least 3-5 different variations. This increases your chances of identifying the offer that most resonates with your target audience.

Don't dismiss an offer too quickly. Allow at least 2-3 weeks to see whether it improves. Make sure you comprehend the information you're gathering.

This will assist you in determining the elements influencing your outcomes.

Use various testing methodologies. A/B testing, multivariate testing, and split testing are some of the testing methodologies available. Each method has advantages and cons, so select the method that best meets your needs.

Gather feedback from your target audience. Make decisions about your offers based on more than simple facts. Get feedback from your target audience to learn what they like and dislike about your offers.

Surveys are an excellent approach to gathering feedback from a big group of individuals. You can utilize surveys to find out how satisfied customers are with your product, what they think should be improved, and what they think about the product generally.

Focus groups are an excellent approach to gathering detailed input from a small number of people. Focus groups can be used to discuss specific parts of your product with individuals and solicit opinions on how to enhance it.

Social networking is a terrific tool to gather real-time input from your audience. You can utilize social media to ask questions, solicit input on new features, and generate enthusiasm for your product.

Customer service is an excellent approach to gathering feedback from those who have already tried your product. You can contact customer service to inquire about their experience with your product, suggestions for improvement, and overall comments on the product.

After gathering input from your target audience, you must analyze it and make improvements to your product as appropriate. It is critical to be receptive to input and eager to make improvements, no matter how minor. You can improve your product and make it more appealing to your audience by making adjustments based on feedback.

There is no one-size-fits-all solution for informing customers about product changes or surprising them. It is dependent on the product, the audience, and the precise adjustments made.

In some circumstances, it may be preferable to inform customers of product modifications. This is especially true if the modifications are large or have the potential to alter how customers utilize the product. For example, if you are adjusting the price of your product, you must notify customers ahead of time.

In other circumstances, it may be preferable to surprise customers with product revisions. This can be an excellent method of generating enthusiasm and interest in your goods. For example, if you are introducing a new feature to your product, you may want to surprise your customers with the news.

Finally, the best method to decide whether to inform consumers about product changes or surprise them is to examine the specific situation and what you believe would be most beneficial.

Finding the proper offer for your target takes time. Don't be disheartened if you don't notice immediate benefits. Continue to test and refine your offers until you find what works best for you.

www.ingramcontent.com/pod-product-compliance
Lightning Source LLC
Chambersburg PA
CBHW050521290526
45786CB00007B/2645